STRESS *hurts*! STRESS *increases illness!* Stress *debilitates*! Stress even *KILLS!* We haven't an answer to *eliminate* stress but we do have a way to *manage* stress!

Living to a ripe old age is certainly something we all covet. Being alive and *pain free* is even better. Because of the additives and preservatives in our food, we are *forced* to grow our own or look for an alternate route. Thus, the health industry is flourishing. People who sell vitamins, food supplements and medicines are raking in the money.

But, what most don't realize is that STRESS is responsible for more than 80% of all illnesses. Think about it—simple, everyday *stress.* So, with reasoning, if we can *manage* stress, we can eliminate 80% of the cost of staying healthy.

For more than four decades Russians have been experimenting with a series of natural foods that would make their Cosmonauts, Olympic athletes, their military and the Bolshoi dancers stronger and more able to manage stress.

If you would like to reduce or **manage** *your* **stress,** an exclusive ADAPTOGEN formula is now available. This is the greatest discovery since vitamins. The Russians kept it a secret. But now *we have that secret!*

Managing Stress

Through the Magic of Adaptogens
(Nature's BEST KEPT secret)

by

PETE BILLAC

FOREWORD BY

DR. KEN KROLL, M.D., FICS

Swan Publishing

Author: Pete Billac
Editors: Dr. Ken Kroll
          Kimberly Morrison
          Sharon Davis
          Melinda Wallace
Cover Design: John Gilmore

Other books by Pete Billac:

The Acquiescent Wanderer
The Annihilator
How Not To Be Lonely
How Not To Be Lonely—Tonight
The Last Medal of Honor
New Father's Baby Guide
Lose Fat While You Sleep
Willie the Wisp
All About Cruises
The New Millionaires

1st Printing - August, 1999
2nd Printing - September, 1999
3rd Printing - January, 2000

Copyright @ August 1999
Pete Billac and Swan Publishing
Library of Congress Catalog Card #99-65296
ISBN# 0-943629-42-X

Managing Stress, is available in quantity discounts through Swan Publishing, 126 Live Oak, Alvin, TX 77511. (281) 388-2547 or Fax (281) 585-3738.
                Printed in the United States of America.

DEDICATION

I dedicate this book to Roy Speer and to his
commitment to help the human race.

And to Dr. Israel Brekhman,
The "Father of Adaptogens."

FOREWORD
(From a talk by Dr. Ken Kroll M.D., FICS)

Dr. Kroll is a medical doctor and a board-certified specialist in surgery. He is a graduate of Rutgers University, Harvard Medical School, and finished surgery specialty training at Stanford Medical Center.

Dr. Kroll is a member of the American Medical Association, the American Urological Association, and the American Academy of Anti-Aging Medicine. He was elected a Fellow of the International College of Surgeons in 1994, and became a Diplomat of the American Board of Anti Aging Medicine in 1998. He ran a hospital for native tribes people in the Central Highlands province of Formosa Free China for World Vision Incorporated. Presently, he is a lecturer and consultant to the Natural Products Industry.

The following message from Dr. Ken Kroll was so direct and so profound that I could find no better words with which to tell the contents of this book. He begins his speech like this:

"I want to talk about a subject so important that the quality of your health—your life—depends upon it. The subject is stress.

"Stress has long-term damaging effects on our bodies not unlike an auto engine. After so many miles, especially without proper maintenance, it starts to wear out. It begins to burn more oil, loses power and starts to fall apart. Stress does the same thing to the human body.

"Some simple examples of stress are the anxiety a person feels when their child is so sick they

start to fear for their life; it's the energy-draining fear when you feel you might lose your job; it's the depression you experience when divorce damages your self-image and your home; it's that heart-pounding, gasping-for-breath feeling when you narrowly miss a head-on crash knowing it would have killed you.

"Stress comes at each of us in a never-ending assault that changes our lives, damages us emotionally and, in ways we now understand, does real physical damage as well.

"The good news is that there now exists an all-natural plant extract of rare herbs called Adaptogens which can block the damaging effects of stress and restore balance to our complex cell and organ systems.

"Adaptogens work on the cellular level and are the most remarkable health-restoring substances I've ever witnessed. Everyone, no matter what their health challenge, should find genuine improved health by adding this herbal food supplement to their daily diet.

"This herbal extract was developed by Dr.'s Israel and Margaret Brekhman with the aid of several hundred top Russian scientists between 1950 and 1990 and is now sold in this country as Prime One®."

Dr. Ken Kroll, M.D., FICS

INTRODUCTION BY THE AUTHOR

I am neither a scientist nor physician, just a writer who finds something "hot" and writes about it. I also edit and own a publishing company.

The information in this book is so very, very beneficial to you that I need this space for you to identify all the "players" because it's a wondrous story and it makes sense. There is no speculation, no theory, no hype, only documented facts by some of the top scientists and researchers in the world today.

I want you to know something about me from the onset of this book in the event the passion I feel doesn't come through in my writing. It is so very important to me that you understand what's between the covers of this book because it could mean so much to you and to those you care for. It could save your LIFE!

I've written 47 books with 38 reaching best sellers status. Counting writing books for others, editing, writing, and publishing, I'd guess that I've had "something to do" with over 500 books.

I write what I like and publish what I feel readers will enjoy and benefit from. Of the 117 books I've published, all but three have made a profit. The reason my books are successful, I feel, is that although I'm college educated, I write like I talk, and I talk in plain language and write as if I were talking to a friend; nothing fancy, just fact.

I try to make a "story" out of what I write. I refuse to write *textbooks*. I try to work with humor because even "serious stuff" can be learned while having a good laugh. Thus, I'm *impaled* by writing critics, school teachers, grammarians and "pure" writers (most of whom have never written a best seller). I really enjoy myself when I write and I want you to have fun while you read what I've written.

Many of these words are not my own, but those of the researchers who discovered these *adaptogens* and those who have tried it with success. This is really *their* story; I'm just putting it in book form and doing it *my way.*

When I learn of something that I believe will benefit others, I research it carefully, perform my own tests with it, and if works on me, I write about it. In this instance, I took these *adaptogens* for about a month and noticed NO difference in anything. So I *sat* on the book but still did research, waiting, hoping for some positive sign. I got my answer in a strange way.

I knew that minds far greater than my own spent years and years to develop these "miracle things" that were all natural and made the Russians perform better in the Olympics than the American athletes. For years the Russians were suspected of taking *anabolic steroids* but none of this was ever proven. And, most of the time, their athletes *were* better.

Now, I'll not open this "can of worms" because the Russian athletes were given the benefits only our *professional* athletes enjoyed but were still called *amateur* athletes. Many of their top performers were "in the military" in that they were fed and housed and taken care of in style; all their government leaders wanted was to *beat the Americans.* It's sad when politics matters to where sports—amateur sports—become a political strategy.

Consequently, the Russians, in the space race to the moon, their quest for superior military strength, their performance in the Olympic games—even their famous Bolshoi ballet—mattered greatly to them so that whatever they could do to accomplish these goals of dominance was paramount.

There is little doubt that many great minds are in the Soviet Union and that "the state" both recognizes and supports those gifted with this knowledge because of this need to prove their superiority in everything they did.

This book gives you *their secret,* the one Soviet scientists kept for so long in their own country and that we now have. *It's exciting! It's miraculous!* It's a medical breakthrough that will change the health and well-being of so many. Unlike the Russians, we want to share this secret with the world!

For the past 20 months I've been working 16-18 hours a day seven days a week writing books, lecturing and traveling. I probably logged more air miles during this time than John Glenn—and I was tired. About four months ago while standing in my kitchen, I felt dizzy and I tried to hang onto the counter top but eased down and laid in a fetal position on the kitchen floor for about three minutes before crawling to the couch to lie down another 10-or-so minutes.

My heart is strong and, like many hardheaded men, (women, too, I suspect) I never go to a doctor unless I have a bone sticking out. A month passed and no dizziness. But in Canada, it hit again. This time I broke out in a sweat and I was sheet white and had to sit at the lunch table to gain some control before a friend helped me to my room. I called my friend, Dr. Jack Herd, in Pennsylvania, and he suggested I go to a hospital.

In the emergency room, they took some tests

like temperature, blood pressure, blood analysis, and an EKG (they call it ECG in Canada) and determined it might be an inner ear imbalance or *Meniere's Syndrome*. I made it home, looked on the Internet, and treated myself. It said to stay away from coffee, caffeine sodas, and chocolate. The computer was closer than the doctor so I did it.

Two weeks later it hit me again—twice in a week—these times it was more severe. I went to my doctor who urged me to check into a hospital for treatment and tests. After one day and $6,300 dollars of tests, they determined that I had nothing wrong with my heart, my veins weren't clogged, blood pressure was normal, and they sucked enough blood to keep three vampires happy for days and they added that my brain was empty, well, not *empty,* but it showed no signs of strokes or a tumor.

A week later (after I had received an all-clear) I had another attack. What could I do but wait, update my will and let the Lord decide.

After that 5th BIG attack, I began taking *adapto-gens*. I called Dr. Kroll and told him that I could not *feel* a difference and I'd been on these *adaptogens* for about a month. "*Perhaps you're perfect*," he said.

"*Would you write a letter to that effect so I can show it to my wife and mother-in-law?*" I asked. He laughed.

"*Seriously*," he added, "*People who are in good physical shape rarely detect a difference immediately; the difference is what it does **internally** to fortify you against future problems.*"

Well, I respect Dr. Kroll, I like him, he has great credentials but we've all heard this before. I, like most people, want *instant gratification.* And, regardless of my physical condition I wanted to see it or feel it NOW! Finishing more than this introduction depended upon it. In the words of Paul Harvey, "Now for the REST of the story!"

That was two months ago and I am feeling great and NO dizziness! I went for an inner-ear test last week and they rolled me, swung me, shot hot then cold water in both ears, put me in front of some flashing lights and I am BETTER! Hence, I am finishing this book. Dr. Kroll, in his infinite wisdom, was RIGHT! The *adaptogens* HAD to be the reason; I had gone off all the vitamins and formulas I had been on and ONLY used what he suggested.

Maybe it was just *time* that healed me? Maybe it was the Lord? Perhaps He led me to Dr. Kroll and LifeScience Technologies. So, I *became* a believer when, by taking nothing but Dr. Brekhman's *adaptogenic* formula, I am feeling healthier and stronger than I have in my entire life. And now, I'm finishing this book. I was waiting for a "sign" and I feel that I got it.

I am not trying to SELL anything; I just sell books and since you already bought this one I have no reason to mislead you; one book is all you need. I just want to share with you what happened to me and tell you about an amazing discovery that could help you.

I encourage you to read my book and find out how YOU can benefit from *adaptogens*. I wish you good health and a happy life. God Bless.

Pete Billac

TABLE OF CONTENTS

The substances talked about in this book are 100% natural, non-toxic, completely safe and include **no drugs or banned substances.** Each uses *natures own power* to supply the nutrients missing in your fitness, training and overall wellness program.

Chapter 1
A HEALTHY BODY

---◆---

The same as most people in the world, I want the *easiest, safest* way to feel good. I am *tired* of listening to false promises by some person selling a product. I am weary with watching some new idea, some secret of the ages uncovered by accident.

Of course, once in a great while people accidently *do* stumble upon something that will make lives healthier and happier. It happened with *Viagra; a pill* that began as a medication for high blood pressure and when it lowered blood pressure and the men were taken off of it, they asked for it back. *Adaptogens* weren't an accident. Nobody stumbled upon them. They were a discovery all right but not an overnight process; it took several *decades* or research and testing to perfect them. Dr. Israel Brekhman devoted his life to *adaptogens.* His discovery will enhance the lives of many. Let me tell you about . . .

Dr. Israel Brekhman 1921-1994

Dr. Israel I. Brekhman was a world renowned Soviet scientist, physician, pharmacologist, a recognized world authority on *adaptogens,* and former

Director of the Institute of Biologically Active Substances.

Dr. Brekhman in his "Thinkalorium", where his creative thinking was done.

The mandate given to Dr. Brekhman more than four decades ago was, *"Search for the answer in nature."* His quest was to discover what nutritional substances, when added to the diet, would be the greatest help to man in resisting the stresses of life and time to:

✔ Release the wellspring of stamina, energy and vitality;
✔ Banish fatigue;
✔ Raise to new levels man's capacity for work and for play;
✔ Enhance recuperation;
✔ Restore the vital balance in which well-being and *being well* are but two sides of the same bright coin.

To accomplish this seemingly impossible goal, Dr. Brekhman realized he must go where nature was untouched by mankind. So, he left his home in St. Petersburg, Russia, and traveled across eleven time zones in the Far East of Russia to a wild mysterious region of age-old forest, jungles, and mountains called the Primorye.

Wildlife abounded there; deer, wolves, and the great black bear, even tigers and *plants.* The plants were in such abundance and variety and untouched by time or civilization that Dr. Brekhman called this area *"the greatest living laboratory on earth."*

It was here that Dr. Brekhman applied, for the first time in history, the disciplines of world-class scientific methodology to the study of these age-old plants. It was here that he broke the codes of plant after plant and discovered secrets that, to this day, are known only to Dr. Brekhman and LifeScience Technologies Ltd.

With a team of 1,200 biologists, scientists and physicians, Dr. Brekhman analyzed and investigated *adaptogens* in one of the most massive, sustained, and spectacularly successful programs of human (and animal) testing in scientific history.

It took a total of more than 45 years and upwards of 3,000 clinical tests on *hundreds of thousands* of people—men, women, and children of all ages participated in these studies—the populations of entire schools, hospitals, and factories. Even an entire town was tested to get the answers that I will tell you about.

These thousands upon thousands of clinical

studies definitively validated the safety, benefits and astounding capabilities of *adaptogens.*

From his earliest human studies, Dr. Brekhman realized that *stress unchecked* and *hopelessness unrelieved* could *ravage* the endeavors, *consume* the dreams, and *corrode* the days of one's life.

But he also realized, to his immense joy, that the complex substances of his long search was revealing when used singularly, and more often in special combinations—could not only *protect against stress,* supply new energy and stamina, but also could touch mankind in a very special way to enrich and illuminate their lives.

As his fame grew, Dr. Brekhman was called upon by the Soviets to apply his special skills and secrets to their space program for the Russian Cosmonauts. These special supplements restored the natural balance of their body systems and protected them against the stresses in motion, vertigo, weightlessness, enforced inactivity and the myriad of stresses inherent in an orbiting space flight.

The results were so dramatic that he was then called upon to enhance and upgrade the performance of Russian Olympic athletes. His program, his *adaptogens*, more so his special *adaptogenic* **formula,** greatly increased these athletes' energy and strength; generated extended stamina and endurance to new levels; and increased recuperative powers of such magnitude that an athlete could train **longer, more often**, and more **intensively** without experiencing fatigue or overtraining.

There is hardly a Russian sports team or elite athlete who does not use the supplements he developed and owe at least a share of their world-class status to Dr. Brekhman's brilliant work. As mentioned in my introduction, Russian politics dictated a driving force that they had to be best at everything they did.

Adaptogens were used in the United States years ago, but ONLY LifeScience Technologies has the specific *adaptogenic* **formula** discovered by Dr. Brekhman.

His formulation of *adaptogens* brought controlled energy, concentration and focus to master chess players and star performers of the Bolshoi ballet, and to Russian pianists and violinists as well as high-ranking government officials. And, of course, their military used these formulations.

Though honor and fame were bestowed upon him, Dr. Brekhman never forgot his dream as a youth to create a nutritional food supplement that could be used every day—by *all* people—from the very young to the very old. " . . . *a multi-sound, life-enhancing, pure symphony of a formula to make people healthy, happy, and to protect them from stress."*

Of course, the Soviets kept this research *secret.* But, in the summer of 1991, destiny and history came together in the stunning fall of the Soviet Union. Under the new order, Dr. Brekhman was able to come out of Russia to America. This legendary scientist was also an equally great and caring human being.

Before passing away in 1994, Dr. Brekhman developed a whole new generation of *adaptogenic formulas* far exceeding his work with the Cosmonauts and athletes. Now, a company in the United States, LifeScience Technologies Ltd., has acquired the *exclusive worldwide rights* to Dr. Brekhman's formulas and this book tells about them.

I am both excited and honored to be writing about this. As I go through page after page of research and read the successes of these experiments, I'm hoping that you who are reading this story are feeling the same excitement as I.

Yes, I got my "sign." I know, most assuredly, that Dr. Brekhman's formula of *adaptogens* brought recovery and maximum health back to me. There is no other explanation for it.

Dr. Brekhman's work on these adaptogenic formulas represents a genuine scientific breakthrough that enhances and improves health using only natural substances."

Dr. Stephen Fulder, Ph.D.
International Authority and Best-Selling Author
on Health and Well-being, Oxford, England

"I have put the majority of my cardiac patients with diabetes on the products with amazing results. Within three or four days, many of my patients called back reporting higher energy levels than they had experienced before. They reported improvements in their ability to walk and arthritic changes, less pain, and less medication, as well as more energy and more alertness."

Dr. Donald Ware, M.D., M.P.H.

"Prime One and Brekhman's Gold (two of the products) are the most successful, health-restoring natural products I have ever seen. The mode of action is far more complex than any vitamin-mineral formulation. I have seen hundreds of people rebound from serious health problems."

Dr. Kenneth Kroll, M.D., F.I.C.S.

These adaptogen formulations are the newest and most exciting addition to human nutrition since the discovery of vitamins and minerals 50 years ago. Dramatic benefits to my patients have included significant drops in levels of chronic pain and fatigue, increased energy, and the decrease or elimination of prescription pain medications. I have also seen the elimination of Prozac and medication for manic depression (Bipolar Disorder)."

Dr. Robert Odell, M.D.

Dr. Brekhman devoted his lifelong work to the discovery of these new formulas to promote health and well-being. He broke ground into an entirely new area of nutrition, providing the key for both achieving and maintaining good health in a modern age, an age when environmental and social conditions continually *oppose* natural bodily functions.

It is rarely one person who does it all; usually it's a team of people and one "team" member was Dr. Margaret Grinevich-Brekhman, his wife. She is a Ph.D. with a degree in pharmacology. She collaborated with and worked by her husband's side all these years and is still active in continuing research projects as relates to *adaptogen* technology.

Don't you think *it's time* to deal with health issues from the *head* and not from television advertisement or some cute story given by celebrities who are paid to do these ads?

I don't care what Richard Simmons *thinks* is best for my body or the fact that Tommy LaSorda took some diet drink and lost 40 pounds in two months. Look at him now AFTER he *went off* that diet. It's truly *time* we approach our health a different way and use the benefits of modern science.

I like a good story, but when it comes to my health and that of my family and loved ones, I prefer listening to experts who have approached health in a *scientific, clinically-tested* manner, not just *hype.*

Health and well-being are the most precious gifts you will ever have and NATURE provided the nutrients you need to keep them. You need protein—the only substance that can build and replace cells. You need vitamins and minerals—the only substances that allow your body's systems to function properly. The only problem with getting minerals from the *food* you eat is that science has *changed* nature.

Some soils where foods are grown are *contaminated* by additives and preservatives. There can be reduced MINERALS in the vegetables; they may contain pesticides and other soil toxins.

Most vegetables and fruits have plenty of minerals, the amounts do vary somewhat with soils, but modern agricultural science addresses this issue.

Just before Dr. Brekhman died, he said . . .

"It has always been my dream to create a special formula for people to make them healthy, stable, happy and to protect them from stress. All my life I have worked toward this goal and I have finally achieved a breakthrough.

It is a complicated preparation of natural plant materials which are the best and most effective ingredients I have studied in all the years of my research.

These ingredients work together in a combination that derives additional power from the mixture itself. All of the ingredients are gathered in ecologically clean areas, then properly dried and processed in order not to lose the active characteristics we need.

This formula will mobilize the body's potential. In our modern world of stress, we need this protection which makes it possible to be daring and to dream."

— Dr. Israel Brekhman

Now, these *adaptogens* are available to *you!* An American now owns the sole rights to the formulations I've listed in this book. His name is Roy M. Speer, the man behind the company who is offering *adaptogens* to the world!

And, he isn't doing it for *money*; he already has more of that than he can spend. He has made a *commitment*; he is on a *mission*; he wants everyone to benefit from these long-held secrets that worked near miracles on those who took them. He wants to bring as much health and well-being to as many people in the *world* that he possibly can.

He is the person who put all of this into motion and is making it possible for me to tell you about these *adaptogens* for you to make a *knowledgeable* decision to combat stress and have more energy and vitality.

There are people who invent or discover something, then there are those who do things with them, the ones who *"take the ball and run with it."* Now, meet the man who is bringing the entire *game* to you.

Chapter 2

MEET ROY SPEER

It was in the summer of 1983 when Roy Speer owned a radio station in Lake City, Florida, and one of his advertisers couldn't pay his bill. An honorable man, but with no money, he brought Roy a large box of *can openers* as payment; the only assets he had. The rest is beautiful, unbelievable history.

Roy advertised the can openers for sale and sold about a hundred within a few hours over his radio station. He then bought automobile tires, batteries, bicycles, some jewelry, etc. Hence, the beginning of the *Home Shopping Network*.

Mr. Speer's net worth is around one BILLION dollars! I was asked by the president of one of his companies if I was impressed by money?

"I'm impressed with *that* much money," I answered without hesitation and with a huge smile. "That's **ONE THOUSAND MILLION DOLLARS!"** Think of that; a person is a millionaire with one million dollars but a BILLIONAIRE has a THOUSAND million dollars. That's just too much for me to comprehend.

Mr. Speer owns the company that *distributes* these cutting edge products that help mankind, with *adaptogens* as their *sizzle* product. He doesn't need the *money*, for goodness sakes. He wants to help people! He wants this to be his *legacy!*

Yes, Roy Speer didn't just "happen" to become a billionaire; he *trained* for it. He wasn't lucky. *Luck is when opportunity meets preparation.* Roy Speer is a visionary; he is smart and he *makes* things happen. He's done it his entire life.

Roy Merrill Speer was born in Key West, Florida. His mother, Thelma, was a housewife and raised three children. His mom and dad divorced and Roy was raised by his mother and stepfather. His mom worked hard to make a living, and it wasn't a comfortable one. It wasn't easy.

Roy graduated from Gordon Military School in Georgia and then worked his way through college and law school earning a Bachelor in Business Administration from Southern Methodist University in Dallas, and an LL.B., (bachelors of Law and Juris Doctorate) from Stetson University College of Law in Deland, Florida.

Upon graduation from law school, Mr. Speer was appointed Special Assistant Attorney General for the State of Florida. From there he became Assistant Staff Counsel of the United States Labor Relations Board.

Mr. Speer is licensed to practice in all courts in the state of Florida. He is also licensed to practice in the Federal courts in the Middle, Northern and Southern Districts of in the State of Florida.

Yes, in 1983 Roy Speer *envisioned* the way people could shop and he *made* things happen. When he sold those can openers so quickly his mind went into high gear.

He recognized early in his career that *technology, communications, quality products with good value*, and *exceptional customer service* could separate him from all other product retailers. Within just six years, using the power of television, his *Home Shopping Network* had established a new industry and set a record as the fastest growing company in America with more than a billion dollars in sales.

Then, about two years ago, Roy Speer thought about and acted upon changing the way people could live. He recognized that the world's most influential and affluent demographic group—*the baby boomers*—were more interested in their continued health and vitality than any generation that preceded them. He knew they were getting to their *autumn years* and they wanted to grow old gracefully—pain free.

"This has created a trend I call the SelfCare Revolution™. As educated consumers continue to grow more resistant to modern medicine, drugs, and surgery, they are turning to alternative care and natural options," he said.

After selling Home Shopping Network in 1992, Roy Speer has not been idle. Among his vast holdings of office buildings, hotels and restaurants, there is also an industrial park, computer company, record company, a publishing company, a magazine and just too many to keep track of. He has created *scores* of companies worldwide in a variety of cutting edge industries.

His *latest* company, however, is LifeScience

Technologies, Ltd. For this company he issued a mission statement:

"My chosen mission for LifeScience Technologies is to maximize life's potential by creating a SelfCare Revolution™ through an array of state-of-the-art technologies, products, market awareness, merit compensation, recognition, communication, and training.

"LifeScience Technologies is a dream of mine. A dream that includes personal and financial wellness for anyone and everyone who has the courage to dream and dedicate themselves to that dream."

Mr. Speer spent over 10 million dollars just *setting up* LifeScience Technologies Ltd.

Mr. Speer is married to Lynda L. Speer his wife of 35 years. He has three children Robert, who works in sales, Richard, who runs one of his companies, and Lisa, who is a housewife.

So what do we have so far? Dr. Brekhman, research scientist, and Roy Speer, billionaire visionary.

Now let's get to how this all pertains to YOU.

Chapter 3
STRESS vs ADAPTOGENS

Stress is everywhere and it works on different people in different ways. Some of the more common symptoms of stress include problems with *sleep, depression, anxiety, irritability, alcohol, headaches, hypertension* or you're just plain tired all the time for no apparent reason.

Stress-related problems are the reason for 80% of the need to visit doctors. Along with the physical symptoms, the body also has more fundamental *biological* responses to stress.

At the *cellular* level, stress can inhibit the passage of energy through the cell walls. This reduced energy level affects your ability to perform physical functions, and inhibits the proper function of all the body's organs—including the brain.

Adaptogens have a *proven* ability to combat stress in all forms. One of these plants, perhaps the strongest of them all (*Eleutherococcus—you* pronounce it correctly if you can), increases the body's resistance to a variety of stressors. Experiments have *conclusively* demonstrated that this particular plant changes the course of the primary physiological indicators of stress.

Research by scientists show that *adaptogen formulations* allow the body to more ably cope with stress; whether it is daily, extreme, acute or chronic.

I promised not to get "clinical" with you and I'll do my best not to. But, being a nutritional and scientific semi-dunce, I reasoned that if I understood most of this, almost anyone could.

Put simply, adaptogens help the body balance itself. This is a healing process. Everybody responds differently. In the first phase, some people experience some signs of adjustment, such as fatigue, headache or loose stools. This can be a normal part of the balancing process. If this happens, cut back your serving to one half of what you are presently taking. Drink plenty of water.

*As your body adjusts, you can gradually increase your serving portion. Although most people eventually use the recommended serving size, you may discover your ideal serving to be **less or more**, or even at a different time of day.*

*Some people who are highly responsive to adaptogens may feel tired with the recommended serving and need only a **half** serving. Some divide the recommended serving into two portions, taking one in the morning and one in the afternoon.*

*And some people find that **more** works best, particularly people who weigh over 200 pounds or who are involved in strenuous exercise. Remember to listen to your own body to find what works best for you.*

Ken Kroll, M.D.

THE IMMUNE SYSTEM

Studies show that the *adaptogenic extracts* included in the unique formula of Prime One renders vital support to the immune system. Another study revealed that the effects of *adaptogens* show the essential aspects of their control over the nonspecific mechanisms which *protect the body from viruses.*

PHYSICAL WORK CAPACITY

Research institutions discovered that *adaptogens* are vital for enhancing a person's capacity for *physical* workloads. Tests and studies with workers in professions involving intense strain from *physical* work *significantly improve* bodily functions by enhancing the body's ability both to *perform* physical tasks, and to *recover* after strenuous physical activity.

In tests on 655 healthy men (*pilots, navigators, and radio operators*), their *recovery processes* were greatly accelerated following tiresome flight schedules. (It works on jet-lag also.) The subjects' *physiological state* improved significantly within three hours of a flight to levels even *higher* than prior to the flight.

In one long-range study involving *60,000 people conducted over a 10-year period* at the *Volzhsky Automobile Factory in Tolyatti, Russia*, absence and disability were reduced by 20-30% after they began taking *adaptogens.* A 30-50% *decrease* in cases of influenza and a general improvement in health were also noted.

················MENTAL WORK CAPACITY ⟺≋≋≋⟹

Research studies involving various tests of *mental acuity* demonstrated that *adaptogens* also have the ability to increase a person's *mental* work capacity. That is, they increased both the *amount* of mental exercise a person can carry out, as well as the *quality* of that work.

Two of the *adaptogenic* plants in Prime One exerted a strong stimulative influence among test subjects who displayed a great improvement in *reading comprehension, aptitude* and *speed.*

These plants *enhance* a person's ability for *memorization* and *prolonged concentration*. In proof-reading tests, a *decrease* in the quantity of mistakes was observed in 88% of the experimental group, while an *increase* in the quantity of mistakes was observed in 54% of the control group.

Eleutherococcus senticosus, (the *adaptogen* we couldn't pronounce earlier in this book is pronounced E-LOO-THRO-KOK-US CENT-TA-KO-SUS). It increases your mental capacity by *improving reflex action, attention span,* and the *precision* of performed work. Improvement in *hearing, eyesight* and *motor coordination* was also an additional benefit noted in these studies.

PERFORMANCE
ENDURANCE
· REHABILITATION

Adaptogens provide the basis through which people can *build up an energy reserve* to be tapped when the body needs it most—under extreme physical tension and during recovery from fatigue.

When I talk of *adaptogens*, I mean, specifically, Dr. Brekhman's FORMULA OF ADAPTOGENS! Don't go running off to a GNC for **their** *adaptogens* and feel that what I'm sharing with you is the same. It isn't!

Most of the test subjects who were administered Dr. Brekhman's *adaptogenic* extracts rapidly displayed improved indicators of energy and endurance, and athletes showed great improvement in their athletic endeavors.

In another study involving a college baseball team, it was revealed that all four parameters of work capacity showed significantly larger increases when *Eleutherococcus* was administered than the subjects who were given a *placebo.*

After administering another *adaptogen* extract to 140 athletes, 74% of the test subjects obtained their *best results* in a 3,000 meter run.

Observations were also conducted on weight lifters, wrestlers and gymnasts. Based on the data obtained, it was concluded that *adaptogens* **increased** their physical work capacity, **decreased** fatigue and **improved** their general mental and physical state.

In an experiment on *healthy* male athletes, *adaptogens* induced a 64% **increase** in work endurance, while a higher rate of cases consistently showed a decrease without the *adaptogens*.

A world class body builder from Lenoir, North Carolina, by the name of Gene Howell said this:

*"In body building, you need every advantage you can get, especially going up against people who use and have used steroids. Dr. Brekhman's adaptogen **formula** has been the greatest advantage I've ever received in body building."*

I don't have a photo of Gene Howell but I can tell you that he looks like a sculpture. He has placed in the top five in several international physique competitions including Mr. Universe. Drug-free for his entire career, Gene follows a strict training regimen.

*"I **hoped** for a 10% improvement over four months. Instead, I got a **20%** improvement in a single WEEK! My strength, endurance, intensity level, and recovery all improved. I had gains in strength in my entire body."*

Just to give you "lifters" and weight fanatics something to judge, Gene was doing 1,860 pounds, six to eight reps with knee wraps for support and assistance on the last few. Within weeks on his new formula he increased the weight to an unbelievable **2,000 pounds without knee wraps or ANY assistance!**

"Although I increased my intensity level about 15% usually working that hard took longer but now I actually speeded up my recovery time between sets. It helped me lose weight much faster than I ever expected, while at the same time my strength was going up. It's been amazing!"

A study of *people performing physical labor* revealed that when *adaptogens* were administered, *all* test subjects showed an improvement in their general physical and mental states. There was also an improvement in functional indicators (*pulse, arterial pressure, vital capacity, back muscle strength, hand endurance under static tension coordination of movement)* and a reduction in the *duration* of the recovery period in all test subjects.

Through extensive experiments on swimmers, skiers and other athletes, scientists around the world have reliably demonstrated the value of *adaptogens* for increasing stamina and accelerating the recovery processes after physical exertion.

NORMALIZING EFFECT

The *adaptogenic* ingredients of Prime One® and Prime Plus® have an important *normalizing effect* on all bodily functions. In studies of an icebreaker's crew on a four-month Arctic voyage, the normalizing effect on the central nervous and cardiovascular systems was tested and noted. This led to *improved sleep, appetite, mood, general mental and physical state and general enhancement of the functional ability* of humans under working conditions.

In experiments simulating the effects of *extreme* changes in altitude on mountain rescue workers, the normalizing action of *adaptogens* on metabolic disorders occurring under such conditions was revealed. The use of *adaptogens* had a normalizing action on the synthesis of RNA during stress, as well as contributing to the normalization of protein, vitamin and water-salt metabolism.

Extremes in bodily functions like *high cholesterol, low hemoglobin levels, irregular sugar contents* and *abnormal blood pressure* may be normalized with the support of *adaptogens,* which activate and regulate normal and efficient blood circulation. At the same time, the use of *adaptogens* in *no way* disrupts the function of these bodily systems.

·············· NONSPECIFIC RESISTANCE ⟺≋≋≋⟺

Adaptogens increase the body's *nonspecific resistance to the harmful influence of various physical factors,* such as cooling, overheating, enhanced motor activity, increased or decreased barometric pressure, and ultraviolet or ionizing radiation. They have also been shown to increase the body's resistance to the harmful influence of both chemical and biological natures (*various toxins, narcotics, hormones, foreign serums, bacteria, etc.*).

Many facts concerning this kind of universal defense action have been obtained for *adaptogens*. In observations on sailors in the tropics, it revealed that

70-75% of the test subjects showed a *decrease* of unfavorable changes in their central nervous system.

Adaptogens, under these conditions, also contributed to an increase in physical and mental work capacity, alleviation of tension in the function of the adrenal glands and improvement in the functional state of the cardiovascular and respiratory systems.

In *another* study on female vegetable farmers, the body's resistance to harmful environmental factors increased, the general physical and mental state improved, and work productivity increased by 23.5% **after taking** *adaptogens*. They also contributed to better recovery after intense physical work.

Adaptogens also possess an *anti-alcoholic action, decreasing* the desire for alcohol. In one observation involving 148 people, the favorable anti-alcoholic action was noted in 73% of the test subjects in the experimental group.

ANTIOXIDANT
ANTI-AGING ACTION

The following are important paragraphs! I realize it *sounds* a bit clinical, but please, read it carefully and I know you'll understand it. Even I did.

As a part of their normal function, body cells make toxic molecules called "free radicals"—each molecule is missing an electron. Because the *free-radical* molecule wants its **full** electron complement, it reacts with **any** molecule from which it can take an electron. When the free radical takes an electron from certain key components in the cell (*such as fat, protein, or DNA molecules*), it **damages** the cell in a process known as *oxidation.*

In addition to free radicals that occur naturally in the body, they also occur as the result of *environmental* influences. These include ultraviolet radiation or airborne pollutants (such as cigarette smoke) which contribute to cell oxidation and *may* accelerate the aging process.

If you think *smoke* is not damaging, just look around at the people who have been doing it for a while. You'll notice that their *skin* is usually rougher and more wrinkled than most others their age who do not smoke. And almost *all* have a cough they've become so accustomed to they don't even notice it.

Antioxidants (oxidation inhibitors) that occur naturally in the human body and in certain foods may block some of this damage by donating electrons to stabilize and neutralize the harmful effects of the free radicals. *Adaptogens* possess an antioxidant action.

··············· CARDIOVASCULAR SYSTEM ═════

Adaptogenic extracts have a favorable influence on the cardiovascular and respiratory systems, providing important support for people carrying out physical work loads. For example, athletes taking *adaptogens* and working out heavily, experienced a **lower demand on the cardiovascular system.**

In another observation of shift workers in the

Siberian gas industry, the favorable influence of *adaptogens* on the dynamics of the cardiovascular system and its protective effects during *severe climatic and working conditions* were also registered.

Adaptogens render a marked *cardioprotective* effect during painful emotional stress by decreasing excess adrenal hormone secretions and their potential damage to the heart muscle.

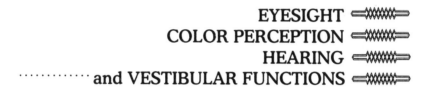

EYESIGHT
COLOR PERCEPTION
HEARING
·············· and VESTIBULAR FUNCTIONS

The *adaptogenic* plants which comprise the fundamental ingredients of these products have been shown through extensive laboratory studies and clinical trials to support and improve the function of the *sensory* organs.

In one study, 111,205 physiological tests were conducted to reveal the influence of *adaptogens* on members of railroad locomotive engineers. The test subjects experienced **improved general physical and mental states, increased endurance, improved headache alleviation and prevention, and decreased irritability,** often associated with this high stress occupation.

The use of these *adaptogens* also led to improved vision, including *increased chromatic stability, improved spectral and contrast sensitivity, improved color differentiation, and increased long distance signal visibility*—all of which are crucial to the safety and effectiveness of people in this occupation.

In another study of 156 people exposed to industrial *noise*, after taking *adaptogens*, all the participants reported a *marked improvement in their general physical and mental condition, an increase in productivity, an alleviation or complete elimination of tinnitus (ringing in the ears) and an improvement in general hearing ability.*

In yet another study on 65 healthy individuals (mainly air, sea, rail and automobile commuters or employees), the use of *adaptogen* extracts led to *alleviation or elimination of discomfort for those suffering from motion sickness and the general discomforts associated with travel.*

These *adaptogens* proved particularly valuable for *sharpening the eyesight and perceptual acuity in skill tests.* In wide trials, these natural substances were extremely valuable for professionals whose occupations make heavy demands on the eyes, ears, and other senses.

In **every** study among pilots, machine operators, Cosmonauts, and factory workers, the sensory functions showed significant improvement under the influence of the various *adaptogens*.

Take into consideration that these tests were administered in mostly *stressful* situations, i.e., factory workers, coal miners, and people exposed to continuous physical and mental labor unlike most of us could imagine.

Their Olympic athletes, Cosmonauts, and scientists were also performing under the most rigorous demands and hardships. Many were subject to continuous freezing cold and the necessity to perform well was ever present.

As I read through this book, I get more excited with each page. I **loved** the *good old days* because we never locked our front door, we picked up anyone who was stranded alongside the road without fear of getting robbed or killed, if someone was hurt in an auto accident we took them to a hospital without concern of being sued, and if I leaned over to touch—even kiss—a small child, I wasn't looked upon as being a pervert or have the child snatched away. Yes, I'm from "the old school" and I appreciate those days and the values they had.

However, of all the things that (I feel) went wrong with the world, there are a great many "new things" that are right with it. For instance, in the time of *Conan the Barbarian* (assuming there was such a person) even Arnold Schwartzeneggar lived only to about 30 whether he was killed in battle or not.

When my dad was young, the average age was 10 or 15 years LESS than it is now and even then, so many lived in pain. I loved the good old days but I also appreciate the good *new* days.

Goodness knows that we are living longer, feeling better, looking better and doing many more things. I went more places in a year than my father did his entire life. My daughter went more places and experienced more wonders before she was 14 than I did at 25. It's a fast world, a different world and in many instances—believe it or not—a *better* world.

Dr. Brekhman and Roy Speer are bringing a better world to all of us if we take advantage of the accomplishments and sacrifices they have both made—for us!

Yes, I am honored to write about this.

Chapter 4

TESTIMONIALS

❖

I appear at meetings, make speeches, conduct seminars, write books, edit books, publish books and I stay busy. I am being interviewed by newspapers, doing radio and televison spots, waiting in airports, getting up early, packing, unpacking, etc.

It has now been almost three months since my last dizzy spell and a sports medicine doctor, Bob Rakowski in Clear Lake, Texas, told me that there is no doubt in his mind that *adaptogens* cured my dizziness. I also have increased energy.

And, as I told you, it MUST work on me in some positive way *before* I will write about it. You heard *my* testimonial in the introduction. But now, I've gathered more testimonials from people around the United States who also have had positive results by taking the *proprietary adaptogens* developed by Dr. Brekhman.

Unlike the celebrities who sign on anything for a buck, these folks are not being paid for their input. They are ones who experienced results and they agreed to share these findings with you.

ARTHRITIS GONE—ENERGY BOOST . . . "I began taking Prime One on September 1, 1998. I had severe arthritis in my back and legs. Feeling as if I had not rested at all, I would begin my day only to be drained of most of my energy by mid-afternoon. Prime One has made a wonderful change in my life. I feel good in the mornings and all through the day, and no more being tired or stressed out in the middle of the day. But best of all, no more arthritis pain."

James Tibbs

HIP AND KNEE PAIN LESSENED . . . "For months I endured persistent pain in my right hip and knee that aspirin would not alleviate. I did nothing other than beginning Prime One *five days ago.* The Pain in both areas has since subsided."

James Stoffel

CAN'T HOLD A CUP . . . "I have arthritis in both hands, primarily in the thumbs. Mornings are really bad. I sometimes could not grip a cup of coffee or even my toothbrush until I had taken my medication. I CAN NOW . . . after Prime One!"

Rosemary Franz

JET LAG . . . "As a coach, I often travel across several time zones with elite athletes who must be prepared for *training and/or competition* immediately upon arrival. In the past, these athletes' performance usually suffered for three or four days after traveling.

During a recent trip to Kenya, I noticed that my colleagues were suffering from extreme jet lag, sleeping for up to 12 hours and taking naps. But that I had the energy to keep going, even stopping off in England and Germany to conduct two seminars without missing a beat.

"I flew over 150,000 miles last year and was still able to function. I attribute this positive change to my using Prime One and Prime Plus."

Loren Seagrave

NINJA GRANDMA . . . Mary Louise Zeller has gone from an over-stressed, out-of-shape housewife to a fit, trim national *Tae Kwon Do* champion.

Mary Louise originally turned to adaptogens to help her training routine. From the onset, the natural plant substance helped her replace fat with muscle. She noticed that the more concentrated versions of it gave her more energy, more body strength and more endurance.

She says *adaptogens* helped her with the intense focus needed to master the complex sequence of movements in which she had to be fluently expert.

This Utah resident is the U.S. National Women's *Tae Kwon Do* champion. But, if you think that's something, here's the really amazing part—she's a 55-year-old **grandmother!**

L OST INCHES—GOT STRONGER . . . "From 1978 until 1995 I owned, operated or consulted with over 100 health clubs. I left the industry in 1995 and my exercise routine at the same time. In August of 1998 I began taking *Prime One* and in September of 1998, I started to exercise again after *gaining* 30 pounds.

"With the new energy that *Prime One* gave me, plus my exercise routine, in four months I dropped from 220 to 195. In January of 1999 I added *Prime Plus* to my daily supplements and a very interesting thing happened.

"By March I had only lost an additional four pounds, but I had lost 3½ *inches* on my waist! My body was burning fat at a high rate and I was replacing that body weight with muscle.

"In December of 1998 I was curling 80 pounds, 36 times. Now I use 140 pounds for my curls. My seated bench press before *Prime Plus* was 110, now I use 170. I am 48 years old and have put together a weight lifting routine twice as hard as many people half my age."

Preston Fields

WHAT'S NEW AT THE ZOO . . . "I have been in the wildlife education industry for well over 18 years, and have a fully licensed and functioning private zoo with over 145 different animals from a varied spectrum of exotic species. Our animals are under a great deal of stress, because they are constantly traveling to many venues, and are hands-on animals.

"We started giving all (birds, hoof stock, and mammals) *Brekhman's Gold,* and *immediately* noticed some great benefits. All of our parrots have started or finished their molt and they have never looked better.

"Our other findings are that our monkeys are also showing the benefits of the anti-stress formulas. They are exhibiting calm behavior and an overall relaxed disposition. Getting the animals to eat the supplement was not a problem."

Karla Majewski
Pacific Animal Productions

RUTGERS UNIVERSITY STUDENT SAYS . . . "When I first got the product it was during a very stressful week. I had finals coming up, projects due and there was a lot of construction going on at the house. I was very tense and very frustrated. I took a capful of *Prime One* about 4 p.m. that evening and by 9 p.m. I could hardly keep my eyes open. I felt my muscles really begin to relax and the tension melt away within a few hours.

"The next morning—and ever since—I start my morning with *Prime One* and I find I can handle stress much better. Even when I am tired, I don't get that *foggy brain* feeling as often. I have also noticed that I can go at full speed a lot longer without getting tired out."

Eric Podchaski

OUR SON WAS KILLED . . . "At age 26 our youngest son Michael was tragically killed, and our overwhelming grief caused tremendous anxiety and depression; we were devastated. My wife and I both had difficulty in sleeping and we developed high levels of GI upset and heartburn.

"After only *three days* on *Prime One*, I noticed that my heartburn was beginning to abate and I haven't had the need for any antacid relief for forty-nine days and counting. My GI symptoms have also abated.

"My wife and I now sleep *all night* and we both awake each morning refreshed and ready to meet the new day without the stomach-wrenching anxiety we had previously known. Our experience with *adaptogen* products have literally and positively changed our lives. Our son's death will always be with us and we grieve often, but we can cope much better with these adaptogens."

Charlie and Delores Schaumburg

SERIOUS SINUS . . . "My physician diagnosed me with *migraine-equivalent sinusitis* a few years ago.

In Tennessee we have a wide array of different pollens that keep allergies in an uproar. Since I began taking *Prime One* daily, I am **off** the prescribed drugs and headache free, and I have more energy on a consistent basis than ever before.

"These positive results have encouraged me to share the product to improve the lifestyle of other people I care about. You can't put a price on that!"

Linda Forrest

DEPRESSION and DIABETES . . . "I am a 72-year-old widow. I lost my husband of over 50 years to cancer last year. Being alone for the first time in my life, I became depressed. I am also a diabetic and have to keep close watch to keep that under control.

"When my daughter introduced me to *Prime One,* I immediately experienced positive changes. My overall health is better and my energy level and outlook on life are at an all-time high.

"Instead of staying home and being depressed, I am out and about. My kids can't keep up with me, and I think more clearly and sleep better. My physician is impressed with how my blood sugar has stabilized.

Sophia Anderson

KNEE SURGERY ... "I have had four knee surgeries including ACL Reconstruction on both knees and spent the last 20+ years of my life with nagging arthritis. After only *one month* of taking *Prime One,* the pain lessened. Within *two months* the **pain was gone!**

"I am now bicycling, walking, golfing, pitching batting practice and doing things that for years have been painful and—I NO LONGER HURT! My energy level has increased and my weight has dropped significantly.

"I added *Prime **Plus*** to my health program and the results have been increased an energy level and weight loss. These are life-changing products."

Randy Forrest

PROZAC and ZANAX ... "Before using *Prime One* I suffered from depression and panic attacks.

Well-meaning doctors put me on *Prozac* and *Zanax*. Those drugs only made my problem worse.

"Within **one month** of using *Prime One* I was able to get off **all** my medications. I also lost 40 lbs. In three months and have kept the weight off for four years!

"My wife Keri also suffered from hip pain for years and I put her on *Prime One* also. Within **one month,** her pain was gone!"

Larry and Keri Lanteri

A SPRINGER SPANIEL NAMED MAX . . . "As the owner of Pet World, a full line pet store I've had for twenty-three years, I come into contact with many animals every day.

"Approximately two months ago, soon after taking *Prime One*, I started feeling more energy, I had a greater sense of well being, I felt happier, and I noticed that I had much more patience and ability to focus than ever before.

"Many of the pets that we groom have various conditions that cause them pain and discomfort, partially due to the effects of stress on their bodies and immune system. I put several of them on *Prime One* and their owners are very pleased with the results.

"One in particular, a springer spaniel named Max, has taken one teaspoon of *Prime One* every day since Christmas. He is an older dog and has had arthritis for several years. His *mom* (his owner) says he acts like a puppy again. He is more playful and he doesn't seem to be in pain anymore.

"Due to the success that we have had with the *Prime One* product, we have been able to interest several veterinarians in our area to become *preferred professionals* so, *now*, they are able to give their clients the benefits of this safe and effective product."

Lynn Lamoureux

I WILL WIN THIS TIME . . . "I am a 3rd Degree Black Belt and member of the American Taekwondo

Association since 1979. At 49 years of age, it is understandable that one loses some of their flexibility, mental sharpness, and speed, all of which contribute heavily to winning (or losing) matches.

"I am currently competing in the 3rd degree division, ages thirty-six through forty-nine. During 1993 and 1994 I was an international top ten competitor and competed in the 1994 Songahm Taekwondo World Championships.

"In my final match I became very stressed and found it difficult to stay focused with all that was going on around me with approximately 15,000 spectators and my family watching the competition. Plus the fact that all of my victories during the past year would be culminating in this next *two minutes*!

"I lost the final match. I was proud to win the Silver medal but have *revisited* that match in my thoughts and dreams many times since.

"I had just about decided that my Silver medal in 1994 would be the highlight of my martial arts tournament competition career. This was *before* I was introduced to *Prime One*.

"I started on *Prime One* in October of 1998 and it has given me **renewed energy levels** that take me back to my thirties. I have **more stamina** and **recover from workouts more quickly** and with **much less soreness and fatigue**.

"I will be eligible to test for the 4th degree black belt in March of 2000 and I have set a personal goal to complete the requirements and pass the test. I have also set my sights on competing in the Songahm

Taekwondo World Championships in June of 2000 and bringing home the Gold medal.

"These goals have been achieved due to the dramatic physical and mental benefits I have previously described to you from using *Prime One* and Dr. Brekhman's *adaptogen technology.*

James Lamoureux

CALL ME *MRS.* TIBBS . . . My husband James introduced me to Prime One on September 1, 1998. I slipped and fell on ice and arthritis developed in the lower part of my back. I had a difficult time getting out of bed, and if I sat down on the floor someone had to help me up. I was also getting tired during the day and oftentimes I would get stressed out before the day ended.

"Since I started taking *Prime One*, **I don't need help to get up!** I wake up in the morning feeling refreshed and just spring out of bed. I go all day long feeling good and I no longer feel stressed out.

"*Prime One* is the best thing that has happened to me. I really feel terrific and—**I no longer crave sweets!**

Doris Tibbs

NEW MOTHER AT 37 . . . "I am 38 years of age and the mother of a 13-month-old son, and I have been taking *Prime One* for approximately six months. I have always gone to bed late and awakened early. My day usually starts at 6:30 and ends most evenings at 1:00 a.m.

"Upon rising I am usually very tired and stressed. Since taking the *Prime One* I get up refreshed and can go all day without being stressed. My lower back pains have also subsided. *Prime One* gives me great energy and also decreases my appetite.

Michelle Shaffer

DR. SAYS DON'T COME BACK BEFORE 2000 . . ."About three or four months ago I sent my mother a bottle of *Brekhman's Gold* and *Prime One*. She has been suffering from intense arthritis pain for some time, and was on various medications.

"Within only a few weeks on the products, she started feeling a noticeable improvement in her overall condition.

"Last month her doctor confirmed that she was doing better than ever, and told her to keep doing whatever it is she was doing. The best news is that the doctor told her **not to make another appointment until the year 2000** and she has **stopped taking the drugs!** Before taking these products she had been visiting the doctor habitually every three months.

"Personally, I have been using *Prime One* for two years and I can honestly say that my overall sense of well being is great, my sleep pattern has improved, and I have seen marked improvement in my general health.

"As a businessman, I deal with lots of day-to-day stress but am now more relaxed than I can ever recall. I take *Prime One* every day without fail, and consider it one of the best supplements that I have ever used."

Eli Kenton

MORE ENERGY . . . "As an acupuncturist I have tried every herb, tonic and food supplement to increase my own energy level and ability to focus and concentrate—without success. After a week of taking *Prime One* I noticed I wasn't exhausted at the end of the day and my thinking was sharper and clearer.

"I am so pleased that I have ordered my first supply of *Prime One* to offer to my patients as well. I am glad to have this tool to better help my patients deal with their stressful lives.

Joyce Lockwood, A.P., Dipl. Ac.

A FORMER WRECK . . . "After having *two back surgeries* in nine months (the last fusion), I was in *tremendous pain*. I had very *little mobility*, I *lost 18 pounds*, I was *depressed*, I *used a walker, wore body braces*, had *difficulty sleeping,* was very *emotion-*

ally depressed and *in bed about 18 hours a day.*

"**Three weeks** after I started taking *Prime One* and *Prime Plus*, I was UP 18 hours a day, I no longer used my walker or body braces, I was gaining weight and strength and getting my life back. These amazing results are all due—without a doubt—from my using these *adaptogen formulas.*

Nancy Tallas

A N EXPERT TELLS HIS TALE . . . "I have been a health care professional for over 20 years and successfully counseled people from all over the country in the benefits of proper nutrition and the importance of taking only state-of-the-art *proven* products.

"My personal experience with *Prime One* has led to a dramatic increase in my strength, deeper and more restful sleep, and better concentration and focus during my hectic schedule.

"I start *every day* with a cap of *Prime One.* It is the most researched, safe, and effective nutritional supplement I have ever found. I recommend it to all."

Dan Epstein

I met this hunk-of-a-man at a meeting in Jacksonville a few months ago and he is, to be certain, one heckuva physical specimen.

I liked him immediately and called him within a few days and asked for photos. If the picture comes out dark, don't blame me—blame him; it's the only one I have and time is running short.

7 3-YEAR-OLD TOP COP . . . "I've been involved in training men and women to improve their physical and mental stamina for law enforcement work. My focus has been mainly on those things that improve and strength-en the life-support sys-tem. I have, personally, never taken *any* type of drugs, medication, or other man-made prod-ucts that affect the nat-ural development of the bodily function.

"I recognize the importance of diet to healthy body response and I am particular what I put in my stomach. This allows my body to respond to *natural elements* when I try something to test its true benefit on my system.

"I went on *Prime One* and *Prime Plus* about three and a half weeks ago. Within but **five days** the effect of these products began to show up in my system by giving me a building feeling of energy. I lift weights at a professional gym three days a week, and my energy level continued to rise with each workout.

"In but **one week** after taking adaptogens, I could go through a *full hour* of gym work with *no* *fatigue* and I have increased the weight level at all my workstations as well as the *number* of repetitions and sets that I do at each.

"After **two weeks** I could do my full workout, then play 18 holes of golf, and then work the rest of the day at home with energy to spare. I found that my overall *golf game* seemed to improve, and I'm hitting the ball farther than I have ever hit it in my life. At 73, it excites me. **These products are unbelievable!**

"I not only have a feeling of energy and well being, but they also seem to be *turning back the clock of life*!

Courtnay A. Roberts
Chief of Police, RET

WORLD-CLASS HURDLER . . . "I am a sprinter and I have been taking your products for about a month now. During that time, my personal best in the 400 meter hurdles went from 49.19 sec. to 48.82 sec., almost a half second improvement. As a result, I am now ranked *10th in the world!*

"In **less than a week** after I began using *Prime One, Prime Plus* and *Brekhman's Gold*, my workouts have gotten easier, my concentration and energy has improved significantly, and I have experienced an elevated sense of well being. The *most important* improvement is the quality of rest I am now enjoying.

"For years I have suffered from restless nights and wake up feeling tired. Now it seems like the more

I use these products the better I feel. I sincerely believe that the products of LifeScience Technologies are on the cutting edge of technology and will make a global impact in the near future.

Kemel Thompson

A DIABETIC TELLS HER STORY . . . "I'm a diabetic who has had leg ulcers due to high blood sugars. I also have a herniated disc with bulging discs above and below them. My doctors said it's inoperative and that I'd have to learn to live with it. For a long time, I have lived in the fog of pain pills.

"Since being on *Prime One* my blood sugars are normal and I no longer take medicine to control it. I used to take two pain pills every four hours. Now I have only taken two pain pills in the last **six months!** I have more energy and I feel terrific."

Debi Mathews

B RONCHIAL ASTHMA and ALLERGIES . . . "I have chronic bronchial asthma and allergies. I am also a diabetic. In order to function, I *needed* to use numerous medications and pumps for my allergies and asthma. For my diabetes, I needed to take *two* medications a day.

"Now, after taking *Prime One* and *Prime Plus* I am down to **one** medication for my diabetes, and I'm looking forward to coming off of my medication completely. My blood sugar levels have dropped considerably, I feel better, I have more energy, I sleep very well and I no longer feel stressed out."

Laverne Joyner

CROHN'S DISEASE . . . "I've had *Crohn's disease* since I was 27 years old. I'm in my 50's now. I was below 80 pounds. Everything I ate ran out my ileostomy (surgical opening in the small intestine to an outside bag), my *stoma* was dark, and my doctor said I would have to be *tube fed* only. I was placed on *guarded condition* and I feared the worse.

"I started taking *Prime One*, and **right away** I felt better and had more energy. Soon I was eating and my ileostomy started to regulate itself! I even slept better!

"After only one week I called two of my friends to come to my home so I could tell them and SHOW them that I was gaining weight! My *stoma* has turned back to pink and has luster. *Prime One* not only *enriched* the quality of my life. It has **given** me life!

Sandy Weatherby

To familiarize you with Crohn's (krone's) disease, it is a chronic inflammatory condition of the intestine which cause intermittent attacks of diarrhea, weight loss, abdomi-

nal pain and fever. There is no known cause; it could be hereditary.

Treatment includes a nutritious diet, painkilling drugs, antibiotics, and sometimes **corticosteroids** *(steroid hormone drugs to relieve inflammation, allergies and rheumatic disorders).*

A COMPUTER TESTIMONIAL . . . "In all my research on the computer (and I really *know* how to use the search engines) I could NOT find anything online to raise a **red flag** with LifeScience Technologies or its products.

"I have hammered *bogus* companies for many years and on the *online battlefield* I am merciless. Nothing is worse, in my opinion, than to give someone *false* hope in order to make a dollar.

"When my beloved wife Vivian was near death, I turned my massive research capabilities onto the health products of LifeScience Technologies. I tried to find fault or falsehood in their *adaptogens* and found **none!**

"My wife had dropped to 84 pounds due to complications with a previous stroke (*she could no longer take any food by mouth*), and her doctors inserted a feeding tube into her to try and pump in super nutrition products to save her life.

"I literally put my wife's life in the hands of Life-Science Technologies products at that moment in time, and my wife's condition **steadily improved!**

"I used prescription nutrition products, but I did

not see the dramatic change in her until I started her on *Prime One* and *Brekhman's Gold.* As I live and breathe this is the absolute truth.

Michael Wimberly

PAIN AND MARY ON THE RUN . . . "I was injured in a severe accident. They put steel rods and plates in my spine and across my shoulders. I'm on total disability and could barely get around my mobile home. I also take a lot of pain medication. Pain and depression were my daily companions.

"I took *Prime One* and started feeling better instantly. I not only *cut down* the amount of pain pills I was taking, but I started walking to the end of my driveway—soon to the next mobile home and back. Before I knew it, I was walking around the block!

" A friend bought me a low rider bike. A few months ago I could never have ridden it, but now I go all over the park. I can even ride in a car. Want to hear my whole story? Call and take me to lunch.

"*Prime One* has done this for me. I no longer just exist. I have a life!"

Mary Eaton

JUNGLE JUICE . . . A young man (his mom never mentioned his age) by the name of Sean Orr has given *Prime One* which he promptly named, "*Jungle Juice.*" Sean suffers from *Systemic Juvenile*

Rheumatoid Arthritis.

"On bad days Sean's joints would swell such that he had to spend *hours* in the whirlpool just to move with minimal pain," Sean's mom, Kathy, said.

"When I put him on *Prime One*, his life hasn't been the same, and this has gone on for over a year!

I can't begin to tell you how wonderful Sean feels now that he's on *Prime One*. He is playing basketball with friends and just being a regular kid. It's amazing!"

Kathy Orr

These testimonials are all true! These aren't people who ***think*** *adaptogens work—nor are they* ***paid*** *to give these testimonials. These individuals offered them as a beacon to help others.*

Chapter 5
QUESTIONS and ANSWERS

Q. What are adaptogens?

They are biologically, non-toxic active substances found in certain herbs and plants which help the body and mind adapt to the changes and stress of life. You've read the amazing results on hundreds of thousands of people tested. They are miraculous.

Q. How do they work?

They help the body help itself by strengthening and making better use of its resources. They work at the *cellular level*, on every cell in the body all at the same time. You see, stress *reduces* the efficiency and vitality not only of the cell itself, but also of whatever body system to which that cell belongs.

Adaptogens combine glucose and enzymes which allow the cell full access to its energy potential. Positive changes in these cells mean healthier functioning of every organ and body system.

Q. What do *adaptogens* do at the cellular level?

Your body is dependent upon the healthy functioning of the cells. Stress has an impact at the cellular level—depriving cells of their energy supply. When a cell cannot function properly, it becomes weak and damaged. The body gradually breaks down as disease and aging processes begin. This is where *adaptogens* enter the picture in a remarkable way.

Q. Do adaptogens work right away?

Yes! From the moment you take them, they allow the cell to absorb and use its available energy by uniting glucose and enzymes. They also prevent the formation of complex molecules which *obstruct* the cells from manufacturing energy properly. When there is no obstruction, the body is allowed full access to its energy potential and the cells remain healthy.

This process actually takes place in every cell in the body. The cells return to healthier functioning as the various body organs and systems begin to normalize. This normalizing effect may be noticeable in various internal or external ways. Ultimately, the entire body will normalize itself and achieve the balance that nature intended.

Q. Is there another drug on the market that works like this?

In the words of former President of the United States, Richard M. Nixon, "*Let me make this perfectly clear.*" Adaptogens are NOT drugs! They are the only *natural* substances which can *help* the body protect itself from stress. They provide benefits which are impossible to get in any other way.

To complete the answer, *No*, there is nothing quite like this as yet. *Adaptogens* are completely unique in nature.

Q. **Tell me about stress and how it affects the body.**

When under stress, the body reacts by producing adrenaline and Cortisol which puts the whole body on a state of alert—chemical signals that prepare the body and mind for stress. The metabolism, blood pressure and circulation are disrupted. Immunity and resistance are drastically reduced. Performance suffers. In short, stress undermines health and destroys well-being.

Q. **How can I get these adaptogens?**

Roy Speer's LifeScience Technologies is the **only** source for this exclusive adaptogenic formula. They come in two forms, a liquid that you drink, or in a bottle with a dropper. I'll tell you about each as we move along as well as where you can get them.

Q. **Do either of these adaptogens remove stress?**

No! NOTHING that we are aware of *removes* stress! In choosing to name this book I would have liked to have had the title read REMOVE STRESS or RID THE BODY OF STRESS but this is not possible. These *adaptogens* help the body *adapt to* stress, and, in fact, BLOCK the damaging effects of stress!

Q. Will you tell me about these *adaptogens?*

Yes! The first I need to tell you about is called *Prime One*. When you take *Prime One*, your *reaction* to stress is different. The response is sharper, but the production of adrenaline and Cortisol (*otherwise known as* hydrocortisone *which controls the level of glucose, fats and water in the body*) slows down and there is more left in reserve. Tests proved that people are not as quickly exhausted fewer hormones are needed to achieve the same effect since.

Q. Will Prime One work on everyone?

From the moment you first take Prime One it begins its work at the *cellular* level. The body limits its own reaction to stress and cells return to a healthy state. This effect happens for *everyone.*

Many of the internal changes are not *felt*—but they are both immediate and dramatic. The way these show up in everyday life may be subtle at first but once the cellular changes happen, people can begin to see or feel the difference in themselves as the body adapts and balances itself.

With as little times as a few hours or as long as a few months, you will ultimately experience Prime One's impact as noticeable changes in daily life; emotional and physical health; and a sense of overall well-being.

Everyone's body reacts differently to certain stimuli but the amazing *adaptogenic* formula in Prime One performs miracles *inside* the body. It works, regardless of what you eat, drink or do.

Q. Are there *recent* tests on Prime One?

Tests were performed on over half a million people over a period of forty years. But RECENT tests were performed from October 19-20, 1994, by Merrill Research & Associates at its data collection facility in San Mateo, California with 204 telephone interviews with consumers who had used Prime One for one year or more.

Specifically, the company wanted to document the long-term benefit of Prime One regarding stress resistance, increased energy, and enhanced performance.

Their findings indicated that nearly all (97%) of the respondents said that they noticed a *positive* change on at least one benefit commonly associated with Prime One. Nine out of ten said they had noticed improvements in at least five areas, with nearly seven in ten reporting a positive change in at least 10 areas. Other positive findings included:

- *88% felt less tension or anxiety*
- *87% felt better able to cope with stress*
- *87% felt more energy*
- *71% improved relationship with their spouse*
- *68% improved relationship with their children*
- *57% lost weight!*

They also reported improvements rather than declines in the following areas:

- *Better sleep*
- *Better mood*
- *More energy*
- *Better overall attitude*
- *Better focus and concentration*
- *More positive attitude*
- *Less compulsive eating*
- *More patience*
- *Less sickness*
- *More productive*
- *Less tension and anxiety*
- *Better control of temper*
- *Better job performance*
- *Better organized*
- *Less recovery from jet lag*
- *Less procrastination*

Q. What's IN Prime One that makes it so great?

It is a 100% NATURAL supplement containing SEVEN *adaptogens*. It is designed to be taken every day and is completely safe for men, women, children, (and animals).

Q. How do you take Prime One?

It's a solution that comes in a 30.4 fluid ounce bottle. Shake it well and take one ounce per day (two tablespoons). A bottle lasts one month. The *first* few days, take HALF the recommended dosage. The serving amount varies depending on your age.

● *Take Prime One before a meal (preferably breakfast or lunch).*

● *You may take Prime One once a day or divide the serving into two equal portions.*

● *Take Prime One alone or mixed with water, juice or milk. Some people especially enjoy the taste of Prime One mixed with grape juice. I drink it straight from the bottle. Few complain of the taste.*

Ages 12-65	two tablespoons per day	30 ml or the top line on the cap
Ages 5-11 **Adults 66-75**	one tablespoon per day	15 ml or second line on the cap
Ages 1-4 **Adults ages 75+**	two teaspoons per day	10 ml or the third line on the cap

Q. How about the TASTE?

I describe it as having *a tinge* of apple/prune juice flavor, pleasant to most people. I refrigerate it; I think it tastes better cold. Of course, there will always be some who gripe about it and would prefer it taste like ice cream or a Hershey bar but, *it is what it is!*

Q. Tell me more about adaptogens.

In laymen's terms, *adaptogens* help the body *balance* itself. This is a healing process. Everybody responds differently. In the first phase, some people experience some signs of adjustment, such as fatigue, headache or loose stools. But, do NOT panic! This only proves that the *adaptogens* are working and this can be a normal part of the balancing process. If this does happen, cut back your serving to *one half* of what you are presently taking for a while.

TRY to drink plenty of water. As your body adjusts, you can gradually increase your serving portion. Although most people eventually use the recommended serving size, you may discover your ideal serving to be less or more, or even at a different time of day.

Some find that *more works best*, particularly people who are under high stress or are involved in strenuous exercise. Remember to listen to your own body to find what works best for you.

Q. What about traveling? Not all motels or hotels have a refrigerator. Do I take this one quart bottle with me?

Why not? Stick a bottle that has not been refrigerated between your socks and underwear and try to keep it from tossing about. When you return, keep it on your kitchen counter top or put it in the refrigerator. It isn't NECESSARY to refrigerate Prime

One, I just happen to like it cold and in the same spot in my refrigerator each day. But once you *do* refrigerate it, keep it cold.

A great substitute is to take along a small bottle of Brekhman's Gold (a concentrate of Prime One). It fits easily in a purse or butt bag.

Q. Tell me about Prime Plus. What does IT do?

Prime Plus is an herbal food supplement in *capsule form* that you can stick in your cosmetic bag while traveling. Prime Plus is an integral part of an overall fitness and wellness program. It has a specific and focused action on the body, and perfectly *complements* the holistic, generalized effect of Prime One. This is what the testimonials proved for those who used Prime Plus.

- *Remarkably improved human physical performance*
- *Increased energy, strength and stamina*
- *Increased performance levels in all areas of life*
- *Decreased the negative effects of aging and stress*
- *Built muscle tissue*
- *Helped the body burn fat rather than muscle*
- *Enhanced dieting by increasing metabolism*
- *Improved anti-catabolic action to protect against break down of lean muscle tissue*
- *Improved recovery from athletic training*

Q. How Does Prime Plus Work?

Youth is the body's physical and physiological

ideal. While the body naturally adds vital lean muscle tissue as it grows, this stage lasts *only until maturity*.

Between the ages of 30 and 60 dramatic changes occur. By age 60, the average person has *twice* as much fat as they did at age 30—and only *half* as much lean muscle tissue. This, unfortunately, is part of the natural aging process.

Prime Plus **protects the muscle from break-down,** encouraging the body to burn fat rather than muscle. More lean muscle means more strength, better endurance and improved performance. Prime One is the first natural, safe, effective solution to solve this complex problem.

Q. Talk a minute about exercise will you?

Exercise is the *best* way to get into good physical shape and to lose weight and keep it off. Unfortunately, not everyone *wants* to exercise or has the *time* to exercise and some just plain hate it! What I recommend is that you have *fun* while you get exercise.

Try canoeing down a country stream. Walk the neighborhood with your wife, family and dogs. Take a hike! Maybe I should say *take a walk in the woods,* on a beach, through the park. *Any* form of physical activity that you enjoy can also be exercise. Do it regularly, have fun doing it or just sit at home, watch television and die early and in pain. It's your choice.

There is just so much any vitamin, mineral, *adaptogen* or new discovery can accomplish. I can tell you the good they do, but they work *better* if you help, like drinking 8-10 glasses of water per day to help flush your system, and to get some form of *recreational* exercise at let three times a week.

These *adaptogen* formulas give you energy—the *will* to become more active. When I'm tired and hurting, a team of Budweiser horses couldn't drag me to do exercise. Just leave me alone and let me lie on the couch, look at any number of sports invented by mankind, fall asleep, wake up and not be able to sleep that night and *stay* tired and hurt.

If you will, allow me to go into a bit more detail about exercise, of which there are two types; ANABOLIC and CATABOLIC.

Anabolic is the *positive* effect of exercise. You see, the body must create new *lean muscle tissue* in order to adapt to the demands made by physical exercise. This effect occurs naturally up to age 18 (because the body is in a natural anabolic state).
Once this phase ends, it is *exercise* that stimulates the body into an anabolic mode. This increases strength and muscle tone, and a more youthful-looking appearance.

I did an audio tape years ago about exercise on people past 50 years of age. It was proven that for those who do *not* exercise, if you *begin* a program to exercise for only 20 minutes three times a week that you can become 15-20% STRONGER. This is phenomenal!

It's the difference in being bathed or bathing yourself, getting up on your own or being helped up by that Art Linkletter chair, walking into a movie or restaurant or being helped—maybe toddling around instead of walking. Yes, exercise is important.

The other effect of exercise is CATABOLIC—the *negative* effect of exercise. Ironically, exercise not only *increases* strength and stamina, but also *damages* valuable muscle. As a result, athletic performance can suffer.

The anabolic/catabolic dichotomy is well known to athletes who constantly search for something to provide an *edge* in performance by pushing themselves too hard, yet prevent the breakdown of the vital muscle tissue they need to preserve their bodies and their strength. This is where *adaptogens* work wonders.

Q. How can Prime Plus help?

As we age, loss of muscle tissue results in the lack of tone and strength and leads to sagging, affecting our overall appearance. This muscle loss may occur as a result of not exercising and dieting, as well as the natural aging process itself.

Prime Plus is the *first natural, safe, effective solution to this complex problem*—the ideal supplement on both fronts since it *maximizes* the positive (*anabolic*) effect and *minimizes* the negative (*catabolic*) effect. It protects the muscle from breakdown, encouraging the body to burn fat rather than muscle.

More lean muscle tissue means more strength, better endurance and improved performance. You also look and feel better and compliments on the way you look (at any age) are welcomed by most.

Q. You mentioned three adaptogenic formulas and you told me about two! Is there a third?

Absolutely! The LAST of the famous three *adaptogen formulas* is Brekhman's Gold; yes, named after and in honor of Dr. Israel Brekhman.

When the pace of life *increases* and the challenges *mount,* it's time for Brekhman's Gold. It will *maximize* the invigorating tonic aspect of *adaptogens* to specifically address the all-too-common maladies—fatigue and lack of energy.

In Brekhman's Gold, the concentration and ratio of ingredients has been strategically altered to give your body an *immediate* mental and physical energy boost. It does this by activating the body's metabolism, mobilizing hidden energy and alertness without the common side effects typically produced by caffeine, synthetic drugs and other stimulants. If you're using Prime One and feel the need to *boost* the benefits you're already enjoying, add Brekhman's Gold to your agenda.

Or, if you want to experience more energy and greater resistance to stress *right away*, use *Brekhman's Gold* for a quick start.

Q. How do I use *Brekhman's Gold?*

Brekhman's Gold was engineered to provide *extra* energy *when used in a program with Prime One.*

Use 10 to 30 drops of *Brekhman's Gold* once or twice a day. Your lifestyle, stress level and the challenges your body and mind face will determine the serving size that's right for you.

Q. How does one decide whether to supplement regular use of *Prime One with Brekhman's Gold*?

Since individuals vary on how one or another substance works on them you have to do your own testing. Use *Prime One* alone if you are generally happy with your energy level, overall body balance and want the highest immune system resistance.

Brekhman's Gold should be considered only if you would like to *increase* your productivity and performance level or in periods of increased stress.

Q. The taste of Brekhman's Gold, being an extract, causes my wife to make a funny face when she takes it. Can she mix it with anything?

Congratulations, and yes! Some guys I know have a wife who has a funny face *all* the time. Have her mix it with any other liquid; milk, (it's GREAT in apple juice) even hot tea.

However, I carry *Brekhman's Gold* in the glove compartment of my car, in my carry-on suitcase when I fly, in my bathroom medicine cabinet, and I have access only to milk, apple juice or hot tea when I'm in my kitchen, where I have yet *another* bottle of Brekhman's Gold. It's wondrous!

Help your wife to get accustomed to the taste; it's so very, beneficial. If she *stringently* objects and must use it in milk, *hot* tea or apple, these will neither diminish the strength nor undermine its effectiveness.

Q. Can Brekhman's Gold be taken in smaller servings on a daily basis for a long time?

Yes! Prime One was created for everyday use for long-term, general whole-body protection. The uniqueness of *Prime One* is its ability to help the body *build up* the capacity of adaptation which is used to overcome stress by enhancing general resistance of the body.

Whereas, *Brekhman's Gold* offers all the body's systems *short term support* to function more efficiently. It's for people who need extra energy and need it today!

Q. Can *Prime Plus* be used at the same time with Brekhman's Gold?

Oh, Yes! These two products can be used in combination for individuals who lead *active, demanding* life styles with *great challenges*, such as athletes at the height of an intense training program or before and after competition, or businessmen who are under extreme mental of physical stress.

Q. How does Prime One and Brekhman's Gold work at the *cellular* level?

What bright questions. Health is dependent on the proper functioning of the cells. Stress has an impact at the *cellular level*, depriving cells of their energy supply. When a cell cannot function properly, it becomes weak and damaged, and the body gradually *breaks down* as disease and the aging process begins.

Prime One and *Brekhman's Gold,* from the beginning, allow the cell to *absorb and use* its available energy by uniting glucose and enzymes.

(Again) *adaptogens* **prevent** the formation of complex molecules which obstruct the cells from manufacturing energy efficiently. The body is allowed *full* access to its energy potential and the cells return to healthier functioning as the various body organs and systems begin to normalize.

Q. How about children and seniors? Can they take Brekhman's Gold?

Yes and *Yes*! Brekhman's Gold is a product which can be safely used by everyone. Children from 2 to 6 years old may take five drops 1-2 times a day mixing it with any other liquid (juice best); from 7-10 years 5-10 drops 1-2 times a day; from 11-14 years 10-15 drops twice a day.

Seniors over 55 should start with 10 drops 1-2 times a day and build up gradually (according to your body's reaction) to the normal serving (20-30 drops 1-3 times a day).

Q. I understand there is ALCOHOL *in Brekhman's Gold*. What about alcoholics and religions?

Traditionally, from ancient times, the alcohol base extraction of biologically active substances from herbs and plants has proven to be very effective. All original *adaptogenic* products developed by Dr. Brekhman are alcohol based/extracted.

The second reason for using alcohol is to maintain the quality of the *adaptogenic* extract as a natural preservative. Using 10-30 drops of Brekhman's Gold extract is *absolutely safe* for children. For persons with an intolerance to even micro-dosages of alcohol, such as recovering alcoholics, we recommend using ONLY Prime One.

Q. What if I want to "push the envelope" and start off fast?

I, personally, *like* this attitude; it's the way I do things. Most sort of *waltz* into the usage of *adaptogens* but if you want to dive into it, it's safe to try and we suggest you follow this program. If you want the *maximum potential* of these *adaptogens* quickly, try this.

To begin, this is one of the most *effective stress-protective, performance-enhancing systems* ever developed. It combines two of the most remarkable products available—Prime One and Prime Plus. When combined they provide benefits that are unique in that *Prime Plus* **complements and builds** upon the holistic, generalized effect of *Prime One*. It provides the edge that is the key to coping with stress and high performance.

ALWAYS start by using *Prime One* for 10-20 days and you can then begin to appreciate the unique benefits of adding Prime Plus as a natural perfor- mance-enhancer. Determine your serving size of Prime Plus based on two factors: Body weight and the challenges (stress) in your life. Let me give it to you.

Servings should be divided into equal portions and taken two or three times per day (10-15 minutes before meals).

Follow this plan according to the Prime Plus usage cycle (10-20 days) with a 7-30 day rest interval. The length of the cycle and rest interval depends on your lifestyle, as well as the challenges (stress) in your life. Use Prime Plus when you *really* need to support your body for a higher level of productivity and better performance. The most favorable time for Prime Plus (for athletes) is when your training program is intense and before competitions.

If you are drinking Prime One for the first time, use ½ the standard serving size for the first 5-7 days. This allows your body to adjust to the new nutrients. Then *increase* your servings to the full recommended size.

Continue to drink Prime One every day during both the usage cycles and rest intervals of Prime Plus.

Chapter 6
LET'S TALK ABOUT DIETS

◆

Just for grins, let's switch gears a moment and talk about something that is in our lives each day —diets. This is not a book about diets, but *stress* oftentimes causes us to eat, and eat, and *eat!*

Besides, diets are such a popular subject I thought, why leave them out? And, since 75% of the people in the world are overweight, and about 95% of the population is overFAT, I'm reaching a vast majority.

I absolutely HATE the word "diet" because we all know that diets do NOT work. Just about every "diet" robs the body of LEAN MUSCLE (and fat), but the body is no fool. When you "starve" the body it awakens and says *"This person is taking food away from me so I'm going to store some of this juicy FAT until it feeds me again."*

In short, most people GAIN weight when they go off their diet and all—*eventually*—do!

A few years ago I edited a book for two doctors who talked of *behavior modification*. This is "almost" the same as a diet, but not quite. What it means is not to diet, *per se*, but to *choose* the foods you eat a bit more carefully as well as the *amount* of food you consume.

Gosh, I'm so weary of people telling me that "their" diet works best and a high carbohydrate diet does this, a high protein diet does that, so I've come to the conclusion that if your diet works on you, *keep on it!* No one can convince you otherwise anyway.

I have a friend, let's call her Pam. She is knockdown gorgeous, but in the past year she has put on an additional 30 pounds. I hadn't seen her for about five months and when I did, she was slim and trim again-stuffed in those tight-fitting pants men love to see women (other than their wives) wearing.

"What happened to you?" I asked. "You look terrific."

"I went on a diet," she smiled.

I waited to hear about this diet. I know that diets just never work, only temporarily. Hardly anyone goes their entire *life* eating *stuff* they don't like and even then, in ridiculously small portions.

"I tried the water diet, the grapefruit diet; I tried exercising five days a week, cutting down on foods and nothing worked. Finally, I hit upon a diet that DOES work. Still on it," she said.

"Tell me about it."

"It's really simple. I eat spinach and boiled eggs and that's it. I've lost 30 pounds in three months."

"How often do you do this?" I shot back.

"Well, for *every* meal," she answered, lifting her chin proudly.

"Do you mean that for *every* breakfast, lunch *and* supper you have a boiled egg and *spinach*?" I asked.

Smugly and still smiling, she nodded. What could I possible say? I congratulated her again at how great she looked, told her to keep on it, and offered no advice.

As I was driving off I thought to myself, *"Spinach and eggs?* For *every* meal? If somebody put a *loaded gun* on the table and that so-called diet, I'd jump for the gun and *blow my brains out!"*

Woefully, many, MANY people are on some type of "diet" and this is what they have to endure. This "diet" business brings in a ton of money. People are always inventing some *secret formula* or a *wish pill* that takes weight off easily.

What I feel you'll like about this book is that it talks about FEEDING THE BODY to make it stronger, to help it to do its miracles WITHOUT diets.

To say that DIETS DON'T WORK is not true! Diet's DO work—but not for long. They cannot, unless we adapt a lifestyle that is pristine that we must grow our own vegetables, breath air that is not to be found, and spend hours each day exercising.

Amazingly, *adaptogens* in a certain formulation can help us lose fat, also. You see, Prime One has the ability to stabilize blood sugar levels. And since low blood sugar (*hypoglycemia*) swings are what cause carbohydrate "craving," Prime One can play an important role in *any* weight-reduction program.

Within two or three weeks of starting Prime One,

most people find that they lose their craving for sweets. Remarkable, isn't it, how many ways these *adaptogens* improve our health!

Before we talk about losing weight (or losing fat), let's get serious and talk about the fact that *adaptogens* alone cannot guarantee total health; nutrition and exercise are also factors. Because of our rapid changing world as far as food is concerned, our way of life has changed also. As far as "creature comforts," we are pretty comfortable creatures.

We no longer *hunt* for our food (other than in the aisles of an unfamiliar supermarket), so it isn't necessary for us to *store* fat while waiting for our next meal to run by while we try to shoot it. We eat (if we so choose) daily, regular meals and have no real need to store this fat; we won't go hungry.

As Americans move toward old age, we lose almost SEVEN pounds of lean body mass per DECADE, and the rate *increases* past age 45! This reduced muscle mass leads to reduced *strength* and aerobic capacity and an INCREASE in heart disease, diabetes, and slower metabolism which means we do not burn off as much FAT!

It's a known fact that it takes more energy to maintain muscle than it does fat. The less muscle tissue in your body, the slower the metabolism. This means you must consume *fewer* calories to maintain your ideal body weight.

Hardly anyone eats *fewer* calories as they get older. We have more money, more time, more sports to watch on television and more truly great ads to entice us to eat junk food. It's a way of life.

From age 20 on, the average person's metabolic rate drops about 2% every ten years. This means that at age 70, you have to eat 500 *fewer* calories per day or you get heavy—maybe fat. And as you get older, you lose muscle and gain fat.

For instance, the average 25-year-old woman has a body fat percentage of about 25; the average 65-year-old woman is 43 percent. For men at 25, the average fat percentage is 18% and at 65, it jumps to 38%.

Since most of the food we eat is processed or refined and contains chemicals, to get the necessary vitamins we need we would have to eat . . . well, we can't eat that much. Somewhere it was noted that we must eat SIXTY-FIVE POUNDS of food per day to get the necessary nutrients for optimum health. I'll bet our metabolism is in a constant panic.

Nutritionally engineered food is the logical step to satisfy the body's need and to help it function to where we are feeling good, not getting fat, and have the energy we'd like.

Chapter 7
ATHLETES

—————◆—————

The chief nutritional advisor to the Russian Olympic team and member of the World Anti-doping Conference, Dr. Sergei Portulagov said:

*"**Russian** athletes, because of adaptogens, have a strong competitive edge over others who are not using them. Our athletes exceeded all of our expectations."*

There simply isn't room in this book to ask for testimonials from the thousands of athletes who have reached their peak performances using Prime One, Prime Plus or Brekhman's Gold but I can give you a *short* list from the Olympics.

Those athletes using *adaptogens* in the 1996 Olympic games in Atlanta earned more medals than 181 of the 197 countries.

**THE FOLLOWING OLYMPIC ATHLETES
WERE
ON ADAPTOGENS**

Weight Lifting:

Andrei Chemerkin
Russia, Super Heavyweight
GOLD

Alexander Petrov
Russia, Heavyweight
GOLD

Swimming:

Alexander Popov, Russia,
100m Freestyle -GOLD
50m Freestyle-GOLD

Track and Field:

Charles Austin
U.S.A.High Jump-GOLD

Kim Batten U.S.A.
400 m Hurdles-SILVER

Samuel Matete
ZAMBIA 400 m Hurdles SIL-
VER

Roger Black U.K.
 400 m Hurdles - SILVER
400 m (Track)SILVER
4 x 400 m Relay - SILVER

David & Karen O'Connor
Equestrain U.S.A.
3-Day Event Team-SILVER

John Drummond U.S.A
4X100m Relay-SILVER

Tonja Buford-Bailey U.S.A
400m Hurdles-BRONZE

Calvin Davis
U.S.
400m Hurdles-BRONZE

Ato Boldon
TRINIDAD
100m (Track)-BRONZE
200m -BRONZE

Mary Onyali
NIGERIA
200m (Track)-BRONZE

Steve Fritz
U.S. Decathlon-4TH

Mike Conley
U.S.A. Triple Jump-4th

Abdi Bile*
SOMALIA
1500m (Track-6th
*World Champion 1987,
a major achievement to
make the Olympic Finals 9
years later

Bob Kenned
U.S.A
5000m (Track)-6th

Kyle Vanderkype
AUSTRALIA
110m Hurdles-7th

MALE

CHARLES AUSTIN (USA)
High Jump
U.S. National Record Holder
& 1996 Gold Medalist High
Jump

ROMAN GATAULIN (RUS)
Pole Vault
Ranked 2nd in the World

ALBERTO SALEZAR (USA)
Marathon - Former World
Champion

SAMUEL MATETE (ZAM)
400 Meter Hurdles
- National Record Holder
1996 Silver Medalist,
400 Meter Hurdles

MARK CONOVER (USA)
Marathon
1996 U.S. Olympic Trials
Qualifier;
1988 U.S. Olympic Team

RICHARD HANNA (USA)
Ultramarathon
1996 Olympic Trials Qualifier;
lOOK National Champion
ROB MUSSLO (USA)
Decathlon - 5th Place
1992 Olympics;
3x World Championship
Team

HITOMI TAKAMATSU (JAP)
Long Jump
Indoor/OutdoorJapan
National Record Holder

TRIOMBE HURD (USA)
Triple Jump - Finalist in
World University Games;
Ranked 4th in U.S.

NICK A'HERN (AUS)
Race Walk - 1996
Olympic Team Member;
1994 Commonwealth

STEVE BRIMACOMBE (AUS)
200 Meters
1996 Olympic Team Member;
1995 World Championship

PAUL GREENE (AUS)
400 Meters
National Team Member

TONY BARTON (USA)
High Jump

PETER OGELVIE (CAN)
100/200 Meters
National Team Member

CLIFF RIGSBEE (USA)
Triathion - 1994
Record Holder Hawaii
Ironman Race Masters

ROGER BLACK (UK)
Silver Medalist,
400 Meter and
400 Meter Relay

JOHN DRUMMOND (USA)
Silver Medalist,
4x 100 Meter Relay

CALVIN DAVIS (USA)
Bronze Medalist,400 Meter
   Hurdles

ATO BOLDON (TRINIDAD)
Bronze Medalist,
100 Meter, 200 Meter

FEMALE

KIM BATTEN (USA)
400 Meter Hurdles
World Champion & Record
Holder, ESPY; *1995* Top
Woman Athlete of the Year
1996 Silver Medalist
400 Meter Hurdles

TONJA BUFORD BAILEY
(USA)1996 Bronze Medalist,
400 Meter Hurdles

YOLANDA CHEN (RUS)
Triple Jump - 1993
World Championship

SHARON HANSON (USA)
Heptathlon - U.S. National
   Team

DIANE GUTHRIE-
   GRESHMAN
(JAM) Heptathion/Long Jump
6x NCAA Champion;
1992 Olympian

INES TURNER (JAM)
800 Meters
1995 National Champion;
1994 NCAA Champion

DARLENE MOTA (USA)
Long Distance Runner
1996 U.S. Olympic Trials
   Qualifier;
1995 U.S.World Champion-
   ship Team

MELODY-ANN SCHULTZ
(USA)Marathon
1995 4th National
Ranking for 50-54 Age Group

MARIA TRUJELO (MEX)
Marathon - 1996
Olympic Marathon
TrialsQualifier;
Mexico's Olympic-
Women's Marathon Team
Gold Medal 1995 Pan-Am
Games

SUE LATSHAW (USA)
Triathilon - U.S. National
Team

SIMONE BROOKS (USA)
Long Jump - US Army
Champion;National Finalist

NICOLE BOEGMAN(AUS)
Long Jump- 1996
Olympic Team Member

JANE FLEMMING (AUS)
Heptathlon
Commonwealth Record
Holder

SANDY DAWSON (AUS)
800 Meters
National Team Member

MICHELLE LOCK (AUS)
400 Meters
National Team Member

MARY ONYALI (NIGERIA)
Bronze Medalist, 200 Meters

GEOFF WEIGAND
Rock Climbing Highest
Internationally-Ranked
Australian

ALEXANDER Popov
Swimming - 1992
Olympic Champion:
100 Meters World Record
1996 Olympic Gold Medalist
100/50 Meter Free Style

VLADIMIR PYSHNENKO
Swimming - Olympic
Champion 200/400 Meters

ALEXANDER CHEMERKIN
Weightlifting
1995 World Champion
1996 Olympic Gold
Medalist Super Heavyweight

ALEXANDER PETROV
Weightlifting
1995 World Champion
1996 Olympic Gold
Medalist Heavyweight

FRANK KLOPAS
U.S.World Cup Soccer Team

DIMITRI KHARIN
Soccer
World's #1 Goal Keeper

VALERI KARPOV
Ice Hockey,
Anaheim Mighty Ducks

VADIM SHARIFUDINOV
Ice Hockey New Jersey
Devils

SERVEI GONCHAR
Ice Hockey,
Washington Capitols

OLEG SALENKO
Soccer
World Cup Record Holder

AUTHOR'S CLOSING COMMENTS

I hope you enjoyed my book. I'm not a great writer—not even a even a *good* one—but I research my subjects thoroughly, I write in LARGE letters, SMALL words (that people don't need a dictionary to read), I write SHORT books and I "talk" to you like a friend.

The New Millionaires works hand-in-hand with *Managing Stress.* I want to help those of you who distribute these adaptogens because you do so much good for so many. As sales aids, these books are ideal. They save you time and most of all they get people calling YOU! Use them in conjunction with Dr. Kroll's tape (What's Killing You?).

Put YOUR sticker with your telephone number on the last page. If there is NO sticker in the book and people call ME, I'll try to put them in touch with those of you who use my books according to your location to theirs. Use the book and use ME!

Get radio shows for me; it WORKS! The topic can be *Managing Stress* OR *How To Succeed in a Home-Based* Business. The *New Millionaires* will motivate and teach your downline, it educates the skeptics, and instructs those who have failed in the past.

CALL for my free information packet; it gives you choices and it is truly a smart NEW way to be successful. If you're successful with what you're doing, stick to it. If not, read what I propose, please.

Prime One and Prime Plus made me and my young son well. Dr. Kroll's knowledge and care saved my life. For those of you who want to work and get rich, I'll help in any and every way I can. Thanks for reading my book. Good luck and God bless.

Pete Billac

ABOUT THE AUTHOR

PETE BILLAC is one of the most sought-after speakers in the United States. He has written 47 full-length books, hundreds of short stories and he makes his audiences laugh—hard. His worldwide best seller, HOW NOT TO BE LONELY, sold over four million copies.

Pete is a maverick; he writes what pleases him. His topics range from adventure, war, the Mafia, and famous people, to romance, love, health and motivation.

He gives seminars for Fortune 500 companies on marketing, at universities across America, and offers his services free to schools where he speaks about reading and writing. He also conducts fun lectures on cruise ships.

Pete is currently traveling the world with THE NEW MILLIONAIRES on how to succeed in Network Marketing and on his newest book, *Managing Stress*. *"This book tells people how to become rich. Making money is great—and easy, too, if you believe in yourself and work smart. God wants you to be prosperous, and to help others along the way."*

Perhaps you've seen Pete on Donahue, Sally Jessy Raphael, Good Morning America, Laff Stop and other national televison shows. He mixes common sense and knowledge with laughter. He charms his audiences, and breathes life into every topic.

"Pete is an expert at restoring self-confidence and self-esteem in others . . ."
Phil Donahue
National Television Talk Show Host

Managing Stress

is available through:

Swan Publishing
126 Live Oak
Alvin, TX 77511

(281) 388-2547
Fax (281) 585-3738
or e-mail: swanbooks@ghg.net
Visit our web site at:
http:\\www.swan-pub.com

FOR PRODUCT INFORMATION CALL

Your sticker here

*After reading this book, please pass it on to
a friend or relative. It could change their
lives for the better—FOREVER.*